Who Was
Robert Ripley?

By Kirsten Anderson
Illustrated by Tim Foley

Grosset & Dunlap
An Imprint of Penguin Group (USA) LLC

To my little dog, Sunflower, who is more incredible than
anything Ripley found . . . *Believe It or Not!*—KA

GROSSET & DUNLAP
Published by the Penguin Group
Penguin Group (USA) LLC, 375 Hudson Street, New York, New York 10014, USA

USA | Canada | UK | Ireland | Australia | New Zealand | India | South Africa | China

penguin.com
A Penguin Random House Company

Text copyright © 2015 by Kirsten Anderson. Illustrations copyright © 2015 by Tim Foley.
Cover illustration copyright © 2015 by Nancy Harrison. All rights reserved.
Published by Grosset & Dunlap, a division of Penguin Young Readers Group,
345 Hudson Street, New York, New York 10014. GROSSET & DUNLAP is
a trademark of Penguin Group (USA) LLC. Printed in the USA.

Library of Congress Cataloging-in-Publication Data is available.

ISBN 978-0-448-48298-9   10 9 8 7 6 5 4 3 2

Who Was
Robert Ripley?

Contents

Who Was Robert Ripley?

By December 1918, Robert Ripley had been drawing sports illustrations for almost ten years. He was used to drawing boxing matches, baseball games, and pro golfers. But now he was stuck. He was in a big hurry to leave the newspaper office.

He had a date. But he couldn't leave until he had the sports cartoon finished.

Ripley loved to collect weird and interesting facts. He kept a folder of them on his desk for a rainy day, when he was out of cartoon ideas. Today felt like that day. He began to look through the folder . . .

A little while later, Ripley finished his drawing. It showed people accomplishing amazing things. A man who walked backward across a continent. Another who hopped one hundred yards in eleven seconds. A fellow who jumped rope 11,810 times in a row, and one who ran backward for one hundred yards in only fourteen seconds. There were some track and field facts, record-breaking times spent underwater, and three-legged racers. These were the fascinating things people did to which Ripley paid attention.

Ripley needed a title. He had drawn pictures

of people who were incredible athletes and others
who did downright silly things. He scrawled
"Champs and Chumps"
across the page, then
signed the drawing
"Ripley," as usual. He
didn't think it was a
great idea, but it was
better than nothing.
Ripley wasn't sure
what his editor would
think of the cartoon.

He handed in the sheet of
paper, put on his coat, and rushed out the door.
He didn't want to be late for his date.

"Champs and Chumps" would become a
popular illustrated feature of the *New York Globe*
after Ripley drew more and more of the weird and
wonderful cartoons. The title was later changed
to the catchier *Believe It or Not!* Readers began

to notice and asked for more. In ten years, Bob Ripley's cartoons would be seen in newspapers all over the United States, and he would go on to become a world traveler and a best-selling author. In twenty years, he would be a well-known movie and radio star.

This is his story . . . *Believe It or Not!*

Chapter 1
Santa Rosa

LeRoy Robert Ripley was born on February 22, 1890, in Santa Rosa, California. Three years later, his parents, Isaac and Lillie, had a daughter, Ethel. Isaac was a carpenter. He built the family's house. Lillie did laundry for extra money. His parents always called LeRoy "Roy."

Roy was thin. He had freckles, and his ears stuck out. His front teeth were crooked and poked out of his mouth. They made it hard for him to speak clearly. Roy was always embarrassed by his teeth.

The Ripleys were poor, so Roy's mother made his clothes out of laundry that her customers had left behind. The kids at school teased him about his clothes and his teeth. His teachers weren't too happy with him, either. He drew pictures during class when he was supposed to be paying attention to his lessons.

Roy drew constantly. The family didn't have money for extra paper, so he used any scraps he

could find. He drew his mother and sister, and sometimes himself. He copied pictures he saw. He did anything he could to become a better

artist. By high school he had developed another talent. He became a star pitcher on the school baseball team.

In 1905, Isaac Ripley died. Lillie now had to take care of fifteen-year-old Roy, Ethel, and baby Douglas. Lillie pushed Roy to get a job to help out the family.

Roy tried delivering newspapers, but he hated getting up early. He soon quit. His decision to quit his first job may have saved his life.

When a massive earthquake struck San Francisco in 1906, Santa Rosa—only about fifty miles from San Francisco—suffered serious damage. At least a hundred people died there, including some of the newsboys waiting outside the Santa Rosa newspaper office to pick up their early morning papers.

THE 1906 SAN FRANCISCO EARTHQUAKE

AT 5:12 A.M. ON THE MORNING OF APRIL 18, 1906, THE GROUND BENEATH THE CITY OF SAN FRANCISCO BEGAN TO TREMBLE. WITHIN TWENTY SECONDS, A FULL-FLEDGED EARTHQUAKE WAS UNDERWAY. THE RUPTURE IN THE LAND ALONG THE SAN ANDREAS FAULT RAN 296 MILES. THE RUMBLING LASTED ONLY ABOUT FORTY-FIVE TO SIXTY SECONDS. IN SAN FRANCISCO, THE EARTHQUAKE NOT ONLY CAUSED BUILDINGS TO COLLAPSE BUT ALSO BROKE GAS LINES THAT SPARKED FIRES.

WITH WATER MAINS BROKEN AS WELL, IT WAS ALMOST IMPOSSIBLE TO PUT OUT THE FIRES. THEY RAGED FOR FOUR DAYS. ABOUT THREE THOUSAND PEOPLE WERE PROBABLY KILLED BY THE EARTHQUAKE, AND HUNDREDS OF THOUSANDS LOST THEIR HOMES. THE SAN FRANCISCO EARTHQUAKE IS STILL CONSIDERED ONE OF THE WORST NATURAL DISASTERS TO EVER STRIKE THE UNITED STATES.

Roy thought about the two disasters that had happened in less than a year: his father's death and the earthquake. He decided he wanted to leave Santa Rosa. Baseball or art—or maybe both—could be the key to his success.

Frances O'Meara, Roy's high-school English teacher, saw how difficult it was for him to write essays and read them aloud to the class. She let him draw instead. Roy drew pictures to illustrate the stories and poems they read in class. Miss O'Meara loved them. She hung his pictures in the classroom. Her encouragement gave him confidence.

Lillie Ripley wanted Roy to get a steady job to help the family. He found a job polishing tombstones but soon quit because it was too gloomy. He told his mother that he could make a living as an artist. He had been trying hard to get one of his drawings published. She thought Roy should be more practical.

Just a few weeks before his high-school graduation in 1908, Roy quit school. No one really knew why. He later told Miss O'Meara he needed to earn money for his family. But it seemed like he spent most of his time pitching for some of the semiprofessional baseball teams that played in the area.

He also drew ads and posters for one of the teams. He may have left school because he felt it was time to get on with being a baseball player, or an artist. After all, *Life* magazine had just bought one of his cartoons!

WHAT IS A SPORTS CARTOONIST?

SPORTS CARTOONISTS WERE A BIG PART OF NEWSPAPERS IN THE EARLY 1900S. CAMERAS OPERATED TOO SLOWLY TO CAPTURE EVENTS WITH LOTS OF ACTION, LIKE BASEBALL GAMES AND BOXING MATCHES. CAMERAS WERE ALSO BIG AND CLUMSY, AND TOOK TIME TO SET UP. A CARTOON, THOUGH, COULD TELL THE WHOLE STORY OF A SPORTING EVENT WITH A SKETCH AND A JOKE. CARTOONISTS COULD EXAGGERATE THE PLAYERS' FACES AND BODIES TO SHOW THEIR FEELINGS AND PERSONALITIES. CARTOONS GOT PEOPLE'S ATTENTION FASTER THAN A WRITTEN ARTICLE. SPORTS CARTOONISTS OFTEN DREW CARTOONS FOR OTHER SECTIONS OF THE PAPER, TOO.

SPORTS ILLUSTRATIONS AND CARTOONS BEGAN TO DISAPPEAR AS PHOTOGRAPHIC TECHNOLOGY IMPROVED. VERY FEW NEWSPAPERS TODAY HAVE SPORTS CARTOONISTS.

Chapter 2
San Francisco

Roy earned eight
dollars from *Life* for
his cartoon. It was a
drawing of his mother
doing the laundry.
That was good money
for that time. He
wasn't sure what to do
next, though.

The summer after Roy left school, Lillie
rented one of the rooms in their house to a writer
named Carol Ennis. Carol saw Roy's drawings
and showed them to her newspaper friends in San
Francisco. The sports editor at the *San Francisco
Bulletin* offered Roy the chance to try out as a

sports cartoonist. If he did well, he would have the job. Roy packed, put on his best clothes, and moved to San Francisco.

There were already many well-known sports cartoonists working at the *Bulletin*. Roy soon realized how much he didn't know. He didn't have his own style. He couldn't tell a joke well with pictures. He needed training. The *Bulletin* let him go after only four months.

Roy spent days wandering the streets of San Francisco. He often found himself in Chinatown, the part of the city where Chinese immigrants had settled. There he could eat good food without spending much money. He could listen to the stories of life in China from store and restaurant owners. He was thankful for the kindness of the Chinese people. He dreamed of going to China one day.

Roy brought his drawings to other San Francisco newspapers. The *San Francisco Chronicle* offered him a tryout. Again, if his work was good, they would give him a job.

Roy signed up for art school. He went to classes in the morning, then worked at the *Chronicle* at night.

His cartoons improved, and he impressed his editors with his hard work. When he was given an assignment, he drew several pictures for his editor to choose from. He created cartoons for every section of the paper, not just sports. The *Chronicle* hired him.

In July 1910, a big boxing match was going to take place between Jack Johnson, the great African American heavyweight champion, and Jim Jeffries, a former heavyweight champion. People called it "the fight of the century."

Sportswriters and cartoonists from all over the country were sent to Reno, Nevada, to cover the fight. The *Chronicle* sent Roy. Other writers at the newspaper weren't happy. They felt that

Roy hadn't been there long enough to deserve something so big. The editors felt he had worked hard to earn it, though.

At the boxers' training camp, Roy got to spend time with famous cartoonists like Rube Goldberg and writers like Jack London. A writer named Peter Kyne told Roy that he should go to New York City. That was where all the biggest, most exciting newspapers were.

RUBE GOLDBERG AND "TAD,"
CARTOONISTS OF THE

REUBEN "RUBE" GOLDBERG (1883–1970) FIRST
BECAME FAMOUS AS A SPORTS CARTOONIST IN SAN
FRANCISCO AND NEW YORK IN THE EARLY 1900S.
HE ALSO DREW POLITICAL CARTOONS, WINNING THE
PULITZER PRIZE FOR HIS WORK IN 1948. TODAY
HE IS BEST KNOWN FOR HIS DRAWINGS OF "RUBE
GOLDBERG MACHINES"—INCREDIBLY COMPLICATED
MACHINES DESIGNED TO DO VERY SIMPLE THINGS,
LIKE OPENING A DOOR. THE MACHINES COMBINED
ALL SORTS OF THINGS (LIKE WAVING METAL ARMS,
SPINNING GEARS, SHIFTING WEIGHTS, ROLLING
BALLS, RUNNING ANIMALS, FLYING BIRDS, AND
BATHTUBS THAT POURED WATER ONTO PADDLES) TO
MAKE A ONE-STEP TASK INTO A RISKY OPERATION.

THE MOST FAMOUS SPORTS EARLY TWENTIETH CENTURY

THOMAS A. DORGAN, KNOWN AS "TAD," (1877–1929) STARTED OUT AS A GENERAL CARTOONIST FOR THE *SAN FRANCISCO BULLETIN*, THEN IN 1902 MOVED TO THE *NEW YORK JOURNAL*, WHERE HE BEGAN TO DO MORE SPORTS WORK. HE SPECIALIZED IN CARTOONS ABOUT BOXING AND FIGHTERS.

TAD'S CARTOONS INTRODUCED MANY SLANG WORDS THAT BECAME POPULAR WITH READERS, LIKE "HOT DOG," "THE CAT'S MEOW," AND "FOR CRYING OUT LOUD."

Johnson won the fight. When Roy returned to San Francisco, he asked for a raise. The newspaper's owner said that he couldn't afford to give him the raise, and Roy quit his job.

Out of work again, Roy decided to take Peter Kyne's advice. He would go to New York.

Chapter 3
New York

Roy arrived in New York City in December 1911. The train trip had taken two weeks. Roy had one suitcase with some clothes, a folder of drawings, and a baseball glove. The fifteen dollars in his pocket was his entire life savings.

Roy spent the next few days walking all over the city, trying to find a newspaper that would hire him. No one was interested, though. By the time he got to the *New York Globe*, the editors saw a cold, tired, down-on-his luck twenty-one-year-old desperate for a break.

The *Globe* was one of the oldest newspapers in the city, but it had fallen behind richer, newer papers. However, the *Globe* had recently begun to pack their pages with cartoons, which were especially popular with working-class readers and immigrants. They decided to give Roy a chance.

The *Globe* had a deal with a company called
Associated Newspapers, which syndicated, or sold,
stories and drawings from the *Globe* to newspapers
all over the country. The regional newspapers got
high-quality material without having to pay a
large staff of local writers and artists. Cartoonists
like Roy got to have their drawings seen by many
people beyond New York City.

Roy quickly impressed the *Globe*'s editors. He
worked all the time, drawing cartoons every day.

The editors even let him write some stories for the sports pages. Everything seemed to be going right for him as a cartoonist.

But he had never given up his dream of playing baseball. Roy's favorite team was the New York Giants. When the *Globe* sent him to cover their spring-training games in Texas, Roy mentioned that he had pitched for semiprofessional teams in California.

Even though he was in Texas as a reporter, the Giants decided to let him try out by pitching in a game. Just as he was winding up to throw his first pitch, he felt something snap. His arm had broken! Roy no longer dreamed of being a baseball player. From then on, he focused only on being a great cartoonist.

He also was no longer known as Roy. The *Globe*'s editors didn't like the sound of the name LeRoy. So Roy began to sign his work with his middle name: "Robert Ripley." His new friends in New York now called him Bob, or Rip. Only his old friends and family still called him Roy.

The *Globe*'s editors might not have liked the name "Roy," but they liked his work and his energy. In January 1913, they sent him on a trip to Europe.

At that time, it was very expensive for Americans to travel anywhere outside the country. Without TV or the Internet, newspapers were one of the few ways people could find out about life in other parts of the world. The *Globe* thought Bob was the right person to show it to them.

Bob traveled across the Atlantic on a big ocean liner. First he went to Egypt, where he saw the Pyramids of Giza. Next to them were a group of Egyptian men playing a game that resembled baseball!

In Germany, Bob watched a sport called Mensur, in which men slashed each other's faces with swords. He saw a boxing match in Paris. He was a typical tourist. He got lost. He didn't speak other languages. Instead he yelled louder in English to try to be understood. The stories and cartoons he sent back to the *Globe* described not only sporting events but also what he ate and drank, and the other sights he saw. He used slang. He talked to readers in a voice that sounded like theirs. The European trip was a hit. The *Globe* got many more readers. Bob got a raise.

Shortly after his return to New York, Bob's mother died. Bob was left in charge of his younger brother, Doug, but he didn't want to uproot Doug and move him all the way across the country. He arranged to have family friends in Santa Rosa raise Doug.

When the United States entered World War I in 1917, Bob drew patriotic cartoons about soldiers at war. The war ended in November 1918, and just a month later, Bob found himself stuck at the office, with no ideas for his next cartoon.

December was always a slow month for sports, with football season over and baseball far away. Bob had always loved to collect weird facts. He kept clippings about strange athletic records in a folder on his desk. It was late, and Bob wanted to get out of the office for his date with a Broadway dancer named Beatrice Roberts. He reached into his folder, picked out some of those odd facts, and quickly put them together into a cartoon. He titled it "Champs and Chumps," and handed it in to his editor so he could leave on time. To his surprise, people liked it. In October 1919, Bob did another cartoon with weird sports accomplishments. But this time it was titled *Believe It or Not!*

Chapter 4
'Round the World

Bob couldn't play baseball anymore, but he cared deeply about physical fitness. He read fitness magazines, exercised often, and became a champion handball player. In 1919, he moved into the New York Athletic Club.

Many of the other people living at the club were athletes training for the Olympics. Because the building had a big gym, it was a good place for single men who didn't need much more than a place to sleep and work out.

Bob seemed to be enjoying life as a young single man in New York City. He went to sporting events, drew his cartoons, and went out to nightclubs and parties with his good friend Bugs Baer, another sports cartoonist and writer.

Then, quite suddenly, Bob and Beatrice got married! The sudden marriage surprised all of Bob's friends. Just eighteen years old, Beatrice was a dancer with the Ziegfeld Follies, the most famous series of shows on Broadway. Bob and Bea had been spending a lot of time together, and in October 1919, less than a year after they met, they were married.

From the start, the marriage didn't go well.

Friends noticed that Bob didn't seem very excited when he talked about Bea. Bob didn't even want to give up his room at the New York Athletic Club! He stayed there while Beatrice lived by herself in hotels. Their marriage was not a happy one.

In 1920, the *Globe* sent him to Antwerp, Belgium, to cover the Olympics. When he returned to New York, he began to look beyond the sports world for *Believe It or Not!* ideas: a man who floated across the English Channel on a mattress!

A man who ate glass or nails! Another who had never shaved! *Believe It or Not!*

In 1922, Bob got the chance of a lifetime. The *Globe* wanted to send him on a trip around the world! The newspaper expected him to mail sketches and stories as often as he could, but he could choose where to go and what to draw.

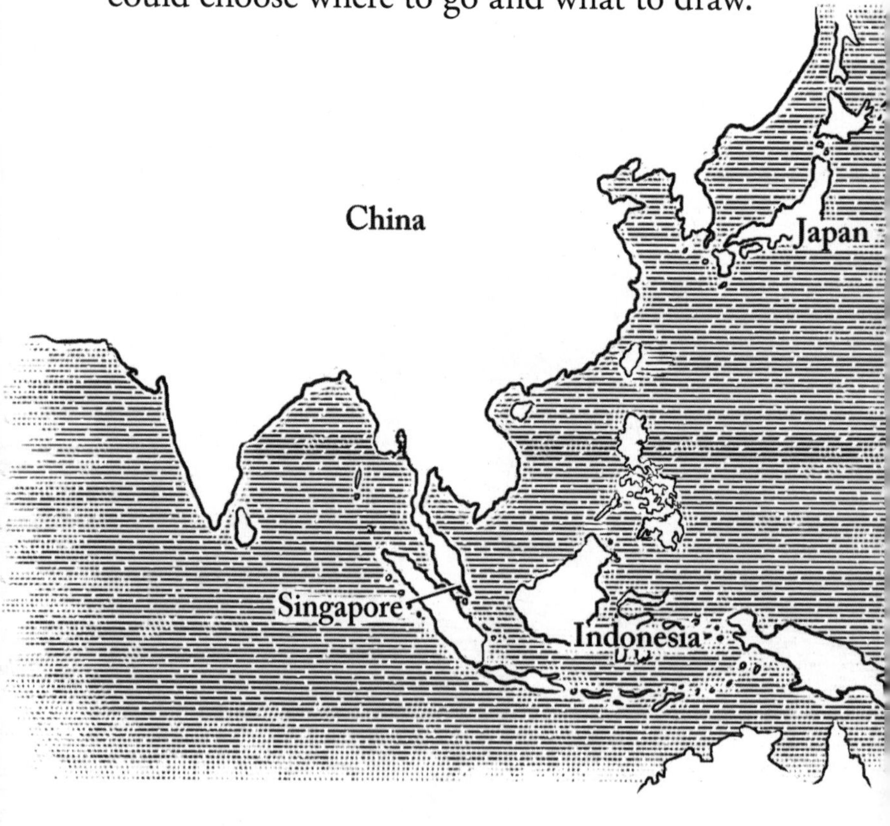

China

Japan

Singapore

Indonesia

Bob took a train from New York to California.
Then he boarded a large ship named the *Laconia*
and sailed off to the East. The first stop was
Hawaii. Bob sketched surfers and hula dancers.

Then the ship sailed for Japan. In Japan he wrote about tea ceremonies and Shintoism, a Japanese religion few Americans knew much about. In China he was horrified by the crowded city streets filled with beggars and disabled people. But he was thrilled by how different the country was from anything he had ever known. He visited a rebel army camp. Angry Chinese soldiers chased him out when they saw him sketching. In India he saw strange funeral customs and beautiful wedding ceremonies. He was fascinated by the religious men who sat on a bed of nails for years, or held their arms up day and night for years at a time. He had thought China seemed strange, but India topped it.

Bob visited Indonesia, Singapore, and Jerusalem. His reports for the *Globe* had descriptions, historical facts, and his own opinions. His articles were casual and fun. American readers loved learning about new places as Bob saw them.

When Bob returned to New York, he was a changed man. His work had changed, too. Now his *Believe It or Not!* cartoons included pictures of the weird, ugly, and sometimes terrible things he had seen. His readers were fascinated by them.

His personal life changed, too. He and Beatrice were finally divorced.

Bob's trip had been a success for the *Globe*. But now the paper had a new owner, who shut it down. Soon after, Bob was out of a regular newspaper job. *Believe It or Not!* was now published directly by Associated Newspapers.

Bob had collected many foreign-language newspapers and books on his travels. He decided to hire a person who could translate them, or rewrite them in English. He hoped to hire someone who would have more unusual ideas to make his cartoons stand out.

NORBERT PEARLROTH

Norbert Pearlroth was born in Austria but lived in New York. He worked at a bank. He knew many languages and loved to collect weird, astonishing facts. Pearlroth began working as a translator and a researcher for Bob. He dug up many new *Believe It or Not!* facts.

In 1925, Associated Newspapers sent Bob on a trip to South America.

He saw the mummified body of the sixteenth-century Spanish explorer Francisco Pizarro in Peru. In Bolivia, he bought a shrunken human head for $100. But South America seemed tame to Bob after his other travels. He didn't find it nearly as strange as China or India!

Chapter 5
Big Time

Associated Newspapers was used to waiting for Bob's drawings and articles to arrive in New York by mail. They would publish them weeks—sometimes months—after Bob had written them. But in 1926, Bob went to England to see the famous Derby horse race. He quickly drew a cartoon of the winning horse crossing the finish line. Then he had someone send the drawing to the United States using a new radio process so it could be printed in newspapers that same day.

The new owner of the struggling *New York Evening Post* saw Bob's Derby drawing and was impressed. He believed that Americans in the 1920s wanted newspapers with flashy cartoons, pictures, gossip, and shocking stories.

Believe It or Not! seemed just right. The *Post* offered to pay Bob more than he'd ever earned at the *Globe*. And Associated Newspapers agreed to continue syndicating his work throughout the country.

Thanks to his foreign travels and Norbert Pearlroth's research, Bob had plenty of weird facts to share. He told readers that if they didn't believe what he wrote, they should write to him. He would prove it was true.

In May 1927, Americans cheered when Charles

CHARLES LINDBERGH

Lindbergh became the first person to fly solo—alone— across the Atlantic Ocean. In February 1928, a *Believe It or Not!* cartoon said that Lindbergh was actually the sixty-seventh person to make the transatlantic flight!

Angry readers complained to their newspapers. They couldn't believe that Bob had lied about a hero like Lindbergh.

Bob explained the cartoon this way: In 1919, two pilots had flown across the Atlantic together. Two helium-powered airships, called dirigibles, also made the crossing. They carried a total of sixty-four people. That made Lindbergh number sixty-seven. Bob had just left out the word *solo*. That made it true. This was Bob's new trick—a cartoon that used very careful wording to make something ordinary seem unbelievable.

These always got reactions from readers. It seemed like Bob was daring them to call him a liar. And he was always happy to prove why he was not.

When Bob was sent by the *Post* to cover the
1928 Summer Olympics in Amsterdam, he took a
side trip to Norway. Norbert Pearlroth had found
out that there was a town in Norway named Hell.
Newspaper headlines read, "Ripley Goes to Hell."
Bob told readers that they should consider going
there, too. He had found it very pleasant.

Pearlroth now worked full-time as Bob's researcher. He spent every day at the New York Public Library, looking for interesting facts about all kinds of strange people and things: A man who could hypnotize fish! A golf player without arms! Pearlroth said, "A really good item is one where your heart has some part of it, where your heart begins to beat."

Believe It or Not! cartoons now carried the phrase "Full proof and details upon request." Bob could prove many of his facts, but not all of them. Most people were okay with that. The phrase "believe it or not" began to pop up in everyday conversation.

A publisher asked Bob to write a book of his collected *Believe It or Not!* facts. When the book went on sale in January 1929, it became a best seller.

Bob's book got the attention of William Randolph Hearst, the most important newspaper owner in America. He offered to have *Believe It or Not!* distributed by his company, King Features Syndicate, then the world's biggest print syndicate. Bob's cartoons would appear in newspapers in big cities all over the country. Hearst agreed to pay him nearly $100,000—*ten times* what he had been making! Three months after Bob started working for King Features, his cartoons began appearing in their newspapers all over the world. The next time Bob went to China, he would be able to find a newspaper with his cartoons in it.

WILLIAM RANDOLPH HEARST
(1863–1951)

WILLIAM RANDOLPH HEARST WAS BORN INTO A VERY WEALTHY FAMILY. AS A YOUNG MAN, HE

TOOK OVER A FAILING NEWSPAPER, THE *SAN FRANCISCO EXAMINER*. HEARST TURNED IT INTO A SUCCESS BY FOCUSING ON STORIES THAT GOT ATTENTION— SCANDALS, MURDERS, AND GOSSIP. HE FILLED THE PAPER WITH SCREAMING HEADLINES, SENSATIONAL STORIES BASED ON RUMORS, AND PLENTY OF PICTURES AND CARTOONS.

BY THE 1920S, HEARST OWNED TWENTY-EIGHT NEWSPAPERS, KING FEATURES SYNDICATE, SEVERAL MAGAZINES, A MOVIE COMPANY, AND A RADIO STATION. HE BUILT A GIANT CASTLE IN CALIFORNIA CALLED SAN SIMEON, WHERE HE THREW PARTIES FOR GLAMOROUS HOLLYWOOD STARS.

IN 1941, A YOUNG DIRECTOR AND WRITER NAMED ORSON WELLES MADE A MOVIE CALLED *CITIZEN KANE*, AN UNFLATTERING PORTRAIT OF A NEWSPAPER OWNER THAT WAS OBVIOUSLY BASED ON HEARST. WILLIAM RANDOLPH HEARST USED HIS HOLLYWOOD CONNECTIONS TO TRY TO STOP THE MOVIE FROM BEING RELEASED IN THEATERS. ALTHOUGH HE COULDN'T ACCOMPLISH THAT, HEARST'S FRIENDS KEPT *CITIZEN KANE* FROM WINNING MOST OF THE IMPORTANT ACADEMY AWARDS, INCLUDING BEST PICTURE. IT IS NOW CONSIDERED ONE OF THE GREATEST AMERICAN MOVIES EVER MADE.

Chapter 6
Believe It or Not!

On November 3, 1929, the *Believe It or Not!* cartoon made an outrageous claim: "America Has No National Anthem." It said that "The Star-Spangled Banner" had never been made an official anthem by Congress.

Americans from all over the country wrote to Congress, asking the government to make the song official. In March 1931, President Herbert

Hoover signed a bill that made "The Star-Spangled Banner" America's national anthem. In less than a year and a half, Robert Ripley, through the power of *Believe It or Not!*, had influenced American life forever!

About three thousand letters a day came to the King Features offices with *Believe It or Not!* ideas. Some of the writers were as tricky as Bob. They liked to see how hard they could make it for their letters to reach him. One sent a letter with a picture of Bob, but no address. Someone else sent an envelope addressed with a picture of a bird made of the words "Robert Ripley." Another sent just a stamp—no letter, no envelope—with an address and a *Believe It or Not!* idea written in very small letters on the back.

Others used codes. Finally the post office made an official announcement that letters with these types of joke addresses would not be delivered.

In 1930, Bob was offered a chance to do a weekly radio show and a series of short films. In the 1920s and '30s, radio and movies were the most popular forms of entertainment. Every night, families gathered around the radio to

 listen to all different kinds of shows—news, music, soap operas, adventure stories, detective thrillers. A trip to the movies always included a newsreel, a cartoon, a short film, and two full-length films.

Bob was nervous about speaking on the radio and on-screen. He worried that his protruding teeth made him difficult to understand. He took speech lessons to help him speak more clearly.

In the radio shows and movie shorts, Bob sometimes introduced the actual people from some of his *Believe It or Not!*s. Audiences got to meet the world's fastest-talking woman, a man who ate a sack of cement, a legless boy swimmer, and a girl who could roller-skate on her hands.

In his movies, Bob showed audiences how he drew the *Believe It or Not!* cartoons.

Bob was a bit awkward on-screen. He spoke softly and carefully. But his curiosity and enthusiasm always came through. Audiences liked him.

The country was deep into the Great Depression. People everywhere were out of jobs. It was hard to find anything to feel happy about. But the *Believe It or Not!* cartoons, radio show, and movies were entertainment that everyone could afford.

Bob introduced his fans to people they would never meet, places they would never go, and stunts they would have never thought possible. He took their minds off their troubles.

Chapter 7
Miles and Miles and Miles

Bob guessed that he had been to sixty-seven countries, and he was anxious to see more. In 1931, he and his best friend, Bugs Baer, traveled by ship to North Africa. They visited Morocco, Algiers, Tunis, Egypt, Palestine, Istanbul, and the Balkans.

When his ship arrived back in New York, Bob did a live radio show from New York Harbor.

The next day he boarded a lifeboat from the ship to a waiting seaplane. The seaplane took off from the harbor and brought him to New Jersey, where he broadcast another radio show. Bob was happy when the stunt appeared on newspaper front pages the following morning.

Bob now earned about $350,000 a year—an astonishing amount of money. He formed a company called Believe It or Not, Inc. He asked his brother, Doug, to come and help run the company. Doug moved to New York.

In 1932, Bob set off on a three-month, thirty-thousand-mile trip around the Pacific Ocean on a luxury ship.

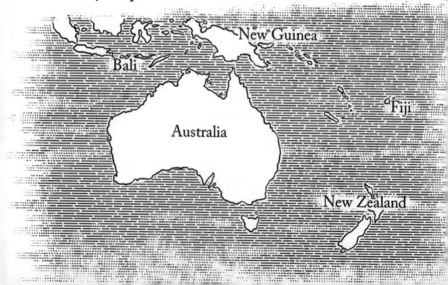

He traveled with Ruth Ross, a woman he'd hired as a translator during one of his European trips in the 1920s. Bob had fallen in love with Ruth, and from then on she often traveled with him. Bob nicknamed her "Oakie," because he liked the way she used the phrase "okey-dokey." He later named one of his dogs "Dokie" so that Oakie could always have Dokie close by.

TRAVEL IN THE 1930s

IN THE 1930S, AIR TRAVEL WAS BUMPY, COLD, AND EXPENSIVE. PLANES COULDN'T REACH HIGH ALTITUDES YET. THEY CONSTANTLY NEEDED TO STOP AND REFUEL. IT WAS CONSIDERED A BIG IMPROVEMENT WHEN A CROSS-COUNTRY TRIP DROPPED FROM TWENTY-SIX HOURS TO ONLY SEVENTEEN!

FOR MOST PEOPLE, LONG-DISTANCE TRAVEL MEANT TRAINS AND OCEAN LINERS. TRAINS HAD DINING CARS AND SLEEPING CARS. WEALTHY,

FIRST-CLASS PASSENGERS PAID FOR FANCY ROOMS
THAT LOOKED LIKE HOTEL SUITES. THE BIG
OCEAN LINERS THAT CROSSED THE PACIFIC AND
ATLANTIC WERE A LOT LIKE TODAY'S CRUISE SHIPS.
THEY OFFERED LUXURIOUS ROOMS, GLAMOROUS
RESTAURANTS, AND ENTERTAINMENT ON BOARD.

TRAVEL BEGAN TO CHANGE BY THE END OF
THE 1930S. AIRLINES BEGAN OFFERING LONGER
FLIGHTS, AND MORE PEOPLE BEGAN TO DRIVE
LONGER DISTANCES IN CARS. TRAIN TRAVEL
SLOWLY LOST ITS POPULARITY—AND ITS GLAMOUR.

They stopped in Fiji, where Bob bought a
"cannibal fork," supposedly used during ancient
ceremonies on the island. They visited Australia,
New Zealand, New Guinea, Bali, Singapore,
Thailand, and many other small South Pacific
islands. Bob was most excited about getting back
to China, though.

But China had changed. Japan had invaded, and the streets were filled with Japanese soldiers. Bob saw Chinese prisoners killed in the street. Stores were boarded up. Buildings had been bombed. Even though the soldiers took his movie camera, Bob still loved China. But the trip was difficult for him.

Bob and Oakie went on to Korea and Japan, then back to California. Bob went to his hometown of Santa Rosa for "Ripley Day." He gave Miss O'Meara, his former English teacher, a necklace from China.

The city's mayor presented him with a roof beam from his old house. When Bob was just a young boy, he had carved his name into the wood. Bob was touched by the gift.

Bob traveled sixty thousand miles during 1932. But, once back in the United States, he didn't stay home for long. In 1933, he set off for Africa. He traveled down the Nile, visiting Sudan and Nairobi. He observed native tribes and their ancient customs.

Bob never stopped working. He did radio broadcasts from the ship during his Pacific trip, and constantly mailed cartoons back to New York. In Africa, he filmed material for his short movies. He was too busy to take time off.

Chapter 8
BION Island Fight

A World's Fair was set to take place in Chicago in 1933. C. C. Pyle, a businessman from Santa Rosa, contacted Bob with an idea. Why not run a *Believe It or Not!* exhibit at the fair? Bob liked it. He came up with the name: the Ripley *Believe It or Not!* Odditorium.

Visitors to the exhibit saw a man who lifted weights from hooks that were attached to his eyelids! Another who stuffed his mouth with four golf balls and a baseball! A twenty-one-instrument, one-man orchestra!

Bob didn't see much of the World's Fair, though. He was traveling again. He and his cameraman drove through Palestine (now Israel) and Syria.

They went to Persia (now Iraq and Iran). A tour
guide took them to a spot many people believed
to be the actual location of the Garden of Eden in
the Bible. It turned out to be a dusty patch of dry
earth next to the Euphrates River.

Next Bob spent a month touring the Soviet Union. Guards kept them waiting for hours at the border. The trains were slow and dirty. He was happy to head home.

Bob decided it was finally time to move out of the New York Athletic Club. He bought a house in Mamaroneck, a town just outside New York City. The house was on a small private island in the Long Island Sound. He named it "BION Island," for *Believe It Or Not.*

Bob now had plenty of room to show off the
many items he had collected during his travels.
Oakie helped him organize and display all his
things. Visitors to his house were dazzled by what
they saw: A room full of Aztec masks! Mastodon
tusks, skeletons, and a fish that swam backward!
The shell of a "man-eating clam"! A life-size
Buddha, and a medieval torture machine!

One of Bob's favorite items was a wooden statue made by a Japanese artist named Masakichi. When Masakichi found out he was dying, he decided to make a life-size statue of himself. He surrounded himself with mirrors as he

carved so he could capture every line and mark on his body. He drilled holes into the head of the statue and filled them with strands of his own hair. The statue looked incredibly realistic. Bob loved to hide the statue in guests' rooms to scare them.

His housekeeper once said that "the most unusual thing in the house is Mr. Ripley." Bob probably agreed.

Chapter 9
Radio King

In 1934, Bob's radio show added sixteen translators. They stood at microphones during the show and translated everything Bob said so that audiences around the world could listen to *Believe It or Not!* in their own languages. He also added a studio orchestra to keep things lively.

CHARLES M. SCHULZ (1922–2000)

IN 1937, ROBERT RIPLEY RECEIVED A LETTER FROM A YOUNG MINNESOTA BOY. HE TOLD ABOUT HOW HIS DOG, SPIKE, WOULD EAT GLASS AND NEEDLES AND YET REMAINED UNHARMED. THE DOG SEEMED TO BE PERFECTLY FINE. THE BOY INCLUDED A DRAWING OF HIS DOG.

RIPLEY LIKED THE LETTER AND USED IT, DRAWING AND ALL, IN HIS FEBRUARY 22, 1937, *BELIEVE IT OR NOT!* CARTOON. THE BOY HAD SIGNED HIS DRAWING "SPARKY," BUT HIS REAL NAME WAS CHARLES M. SCHULZ.

SCHULZ GREW UP TO CREATE THE *PEANUTS* COMIC STRIP. HIS DOG, SPIKE, WAS THE INSPIRATION FOR THE FAMOUS CHARACTER CALLED

SNOOPY. *PEANUTS* FEATURED A SHY BOY NAMED
CHARLIE BROWN, WHO WAS MUCH LIKE "SPARKY"
SCHULZ HIMSELF. IN LATER COMIC STRIPS, SPIKE
WAS MENTIONED AS A COUSIN OF SNOOPY.

CHARLES M. SCHULZ IS CONSIDERED TO BE
ONE OF THE MOST INFLUENTIAL CARTOONISTS OF
ALL TIME.

The show, along with Bob's popularity, was always expanding. In 1936, a poll asked the Boys Club of New York whose job they would most like to have. Most of them wanted Bob Ripley's job! They liked that he traveled a lot and got to meet interesting people.

But the competition for *Believe It or Not!* was also growing. Cartoons and comic books with titles like *Strange As It Seems* and *Weird Tales* also told stories of weird but true things.

In 1937, the radio show became even longer and better. It included reenactments of *Believe It or Not!*s and interviews with real people from the cartoons. The most popular stories featured reunions between long-lost family members or friends. Bob was a good listener. And he always seemed like he cared about people's stories and reunions. He made the people who appeared on *Believe It or Not!* feel important. Audiences liked that. And they could also understand him better!

Bob's manager, Doug Storer, had finally persuaded
him to get his bad teeth fixed so that he could
speak more clearly.

Bob wanted to travel
more, but World War II
was beginning in Europe.
He managed quick trips to
the Caribbean and South
America, but that was as far as he could go.

He started a new radio show in 1939 called *See
America First with Bob Ripley*. He did live shows
from unusual places all over the United States:
underground in Carlsbad Caverns in New Mexico,

underwater at Marineland in Florida, and even from inside a pit filled with five hundred snakes!

Since Bob couldn't travel outside the United States, he entertained himself at home. In New York City, he was always out at nightclubs, restaurants, and shows. He added more antiques and oddities to his home on BION Island. He threw huge parties filled with famous athletes and celebrities. At parties, Bob often played pranks.

And he spent a lot of time with Oakie, who lived in Manhattan but often visited BION Island.

Bob was famous and wealthy. His radio show was a big success. Everything seemed to be going great. Then, in 1941, he lost the love of his life when Oakie died of cancer. Bob was very upset by her loss. When the US government asked for his help, Bob eagerly agreed. He needed to travel again.

In December 1941, the United States had entered World War II. The government asked Bob to help out with a special project. They wanted him to broadcast a series of radio shows that sent positive messages about the United States and its efforts during the war.

The show ran for twenty-six weeks in 1942. In 1943, the navy asked him to do a show about airplanes and pilots. They hoped it would encourage young Americans to want to become pilots. Bob started a new radio show in 1944 with *Believe It or Not!* stories from the war.

Bob now had a big apartment in New York City and beach houses in New Jersey and Florida. He bought an old junk—a Chinese sailing ship— and used it to sail along the Atlantic coast.

Bob's radio shows and houses kept him so busy that he fell behind with his cartoons. King Features Syndicate actually fined him for missing deadlines! After a while, they started using other artists to draw *Believe It or Not!* for him.

After the war ended in 1945, Bob was anxious to get to Asia again, but it still wasn't easy to travel there. In 1948, he finally toured the Pacific.

He visited the Philippines and Hong Kong, then Shanghai, China. Bob had always thought it was one of the world's most fascinating cities, but years of war had wrecked it. Bombs had destroyed many of the buildings. Bob was sorry to see the country he loved changed so much.

Each place they visited seemed to sadden him more. On the way home, they stopped in Pearl Harbor, Hawaii. Bob was shown the site where the USS *Arizona*, a US Navy ship, had sunk during the Japanese attack that had drawn America into the war. More than 1,100 men had died on the ship. Bob was deeply touched by the sight.

Chapter 10
TV Star

Friends noticed that Bob had changed. He lost his temper quickly. He was moody. Doug Storer thought Bob was sick. He was overweight and exhausted. Bob's doctors told him he needed to take time off.

Instead Bob signed up for another project. Television was just getting started in the late 1940s. NBC asked him to do a weekly TV show.

The first TV show was broadcast on March 1, 1949. Bob had a cohost named Peggy Corday. The shows had reenactments of *Believe It or Not!*s, and interviews with the people from them. Bob also

PEGGY CORDAY

sketched cartoons for the audience.

TV shows were performed live in those days. They needed a lot of rehearsal and preparation. It was hard work for Bob. He was very nervous on-screen. He sometimes forgot his lines. But audiences still loved it.

During the May 24 show, Doug Storer noticed something was wrong. Bob stopped talking. He seemed like he didn't know what was going on.

Peggy Corday kept right on with the show, talking until Bob seemed to recover. They made it to the end of the show.

Doug wanted Bob to go to a hospital right away. Bob assured him that he would go the next day.

But instead, he threw a big party on BION Island! Bob didn't go to the hospital until two days later. The doctors told him he had a weak heart and admitted him. The very next day, May 27, 1949, Bob had a heart attack and died.

Bob's funeral service was at Saint James Episcopal Church in New York City. Hundreds of

Bob's famous friends came, and thousands of New Yorkers lined the streets near the church. Then his body was sent by train to California. Bob was buried in Santa Rosa next to his parents.

Bob's friend Bugs Baer wrote a newspaper column about Bob that said: "Nobody ever proved him wrong. If Ripley told me I had two heads, I would go out and buy two hats. And tip them both to the greatest cartoonist in the history of American journalism."

King Features Syndicate chose a new cartoonist to take over *Believe It or Not!* It still appears daily in many newspapers.

Norbert Pearlroth continued to find facts for the cartoon until he retired in the 1970s.

When Ripley's mementos from BION Island were auctioned off, the sale raised half a million dollars. People bid on totem poles, African masks, Chinese pipes, brass dragons, paintings, antiques, and the famous Masakichi statue.

Ripley's spirit lives on the TV shows and Odditoriums that celebrate the weird, the wonderful, and the mysterious. Robert Ripley dared everyone to believe that the world was a marvelous place full of extraordinary people doing extraordinary things.

"BELIEVE IT or NOT!"

TIMELINE OF
ROBERT RIPLEY'S LIFE

1890 —LeRoy Robert Ripley is born in Santa Rosa, California, on February 22

1908 —Ripley drops out of high school just before graduation
Sells first cartoon to *Life* magazine

1909 —Ripley is hired as sports cartoonist by the *San Francisco Bulletin*

1912 —Ripley is hired by the *New York Globe*

1919 —Ripley's first cartoon with the *Believe It or Not!* title appear
Ripley marries Beatrice Roberts

1922 —Ripley is sent on a trip around the world by the *New York Gl*

1923 —Ripley's divorce from Beatrice is finalized
Hires Norbert Pearlroth as a researcher and translator
The *Believe It or Not!* cartoons are syndicated by Associated
Newspapers

1925 —He wins the New York City handball championship

1926 —Ripley is hired by the *New York Evening Post*

1928 —Ripley makes side trip to Hell, Norway, on the way
to the Amsterdam Olympics

1929 —Ripley joins King Features Syndicate, and *Believe It or Not!*
is syndicated around the world

1933 —Ripley's first Odditorium opens at the Chicago World's Fai

1934 —Ripley buys a house on "BION (Believe It or Not!) Island"
Does a radio broadcast heard around the world

1939 —Ripley opens the first permanent Odditorium in New York
Times Square

1949 —*Ripley's "Believe It or Not!"* TV series premieres
Ripley collapses during filming of the thirteenth episode
of his TV show and dies a few days later, on May 27

(102)

TIMELINE OF
THE WORLD

The World's Columbian Exposition (World's Fair) opens in Chicago	1893
The Lumière brothers patent the first portable motion-picture camera and projector	1895
The first modern Olympics games take place in Greece	1896
The Boston Americans beat the Pittsburgh Pirates in the first World Series	1903
San Francisco is struck by a massive earthquake	1906
Raymonde de Laroche becomes the first woman to be given a pilot's license	1910
The *Titanic* sinks after hitting an iceberg	1912
World War I begins in Europe	1914
KDKA in Pittsburgh, the first commercial radio station, begins broadcasting	1920
The Great Gatsby, F. Scott Fitzgerald's "Jazz Age" novel, is published	1925
The stock market crashes and the Great Depression begins	1929
Wiley Post becomes the first person to fly solo around the world	1933
Snow White and the Seven Dwarfs, the first full-length animated movie, opens	1938
The superhero character Batman is introduced in *Detective Comics* #27	1939
The United States enters World War II	1941
The microwave oven is invented	1945
Los Angeles sees its first recorded snowfall	1949

BIBLIOGRAPHY

Hellman, Geoffrey T. "Odd Man—I." *New Yorker,* August 31, 1940.

Hellman, Geoffrey T. "Odd Man—II." *New Yorker,* September 7, 1940.

Leamy, Hugh. "Believe It or Not: Strange Things Under the Sun." *American Magazine,* October 1929.

Ripley, Robert L. *Ripley's Believe It or Not!: The Complete Vitaphone Shorts Collection.* DVD. 1930–1932; Burbank, CA: Turner Entertainment: Distributed by Warner Bros. Entertainment, 2010.

Thompson, Neal. **A Curious Man: The Strange and Brilliant Life of Robert "Believe It or Not!" Ripley**. New York: Crown, 2013.